The Haiku Guide to Cruising

The Pacific Northwest

Sally Stiles

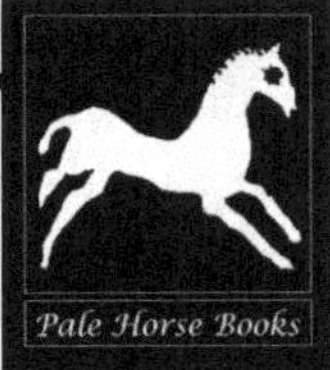

Photographs by Sally and David Stiles

Library of Congress Control Number: Pending
ISBN 978-1-939917-25-6

Printed in
The United States of America

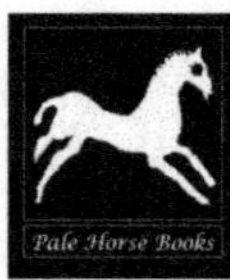

www.palehorsebooks.com

Other books by Sally Stiles available through
Pale Horse Books, Barnes & Noble and Amazon.com:
Like a Mask Dancing, a story of Tanzania
Plunge! A Memoir
The Haiku Guide to Williamsburg
Crazeman in the Bottle
Haiku Guide to the Inside Passage

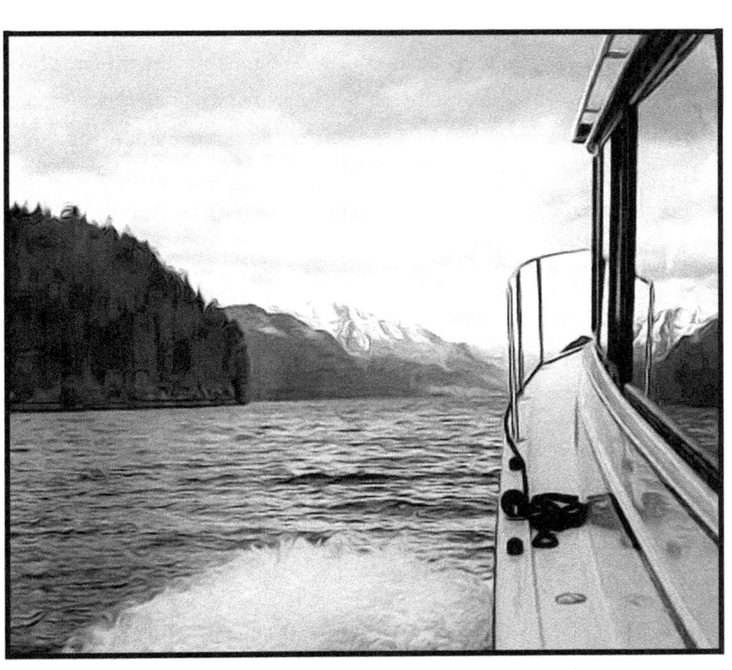

Dedicated to
the searcher
the finder
the sailor
the poet
the dreamer
within you

This slim volume is a celebration of aha! moments aboard our 28-foot Canadian-built trawler, Haiku. The journey depicted is a 1700 nautical-mile cruise from Washington State's Puget Sound through the San Juan Islands, the Canadian Gulf Islands, up Alaska's Lynn Canal to Skagway, across the Icy Strait to Glacier Bay, into the Pacific Ocean to Sitka then through Peril Strait before turning toward home.

The photographs, which my husband, David, and I took, were enhanced digitally, and are meant to visually enrich the poetic images.

Haiku is an ancient Japanese form of verse which uses as few words as possible (not necessarily 3 lines and 17 syllables) to create an impression that distills a moment and induces contemplation.

This volume is a companion to the 2006 book, Haiku Guide to the Inside Passage (revised 2013).

Enjoy the cruise!

Sally Stiles

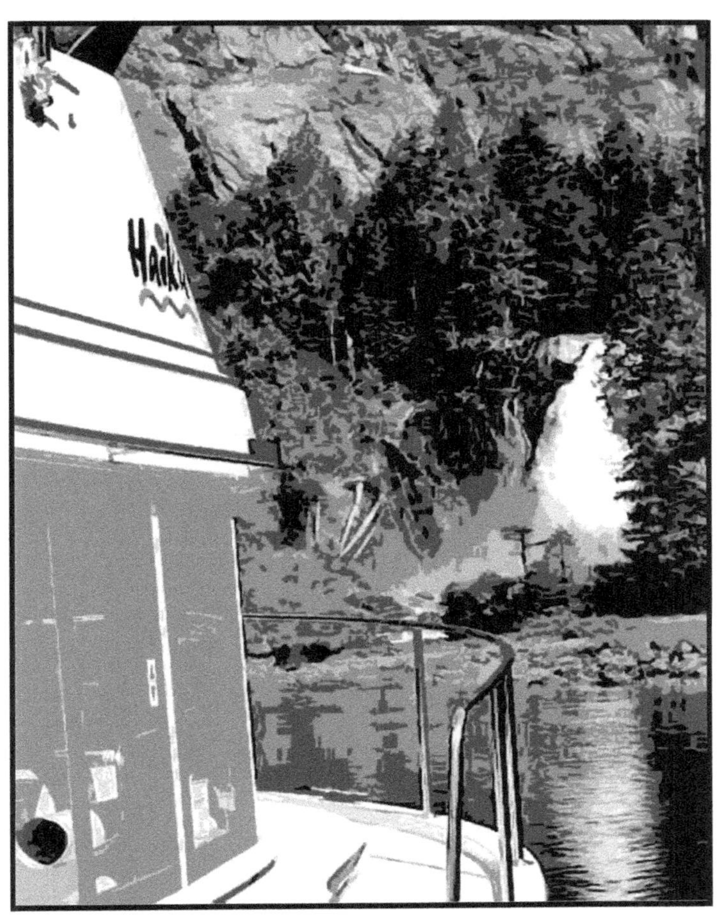

raptors, a pair–
morning rises
through overcast skies

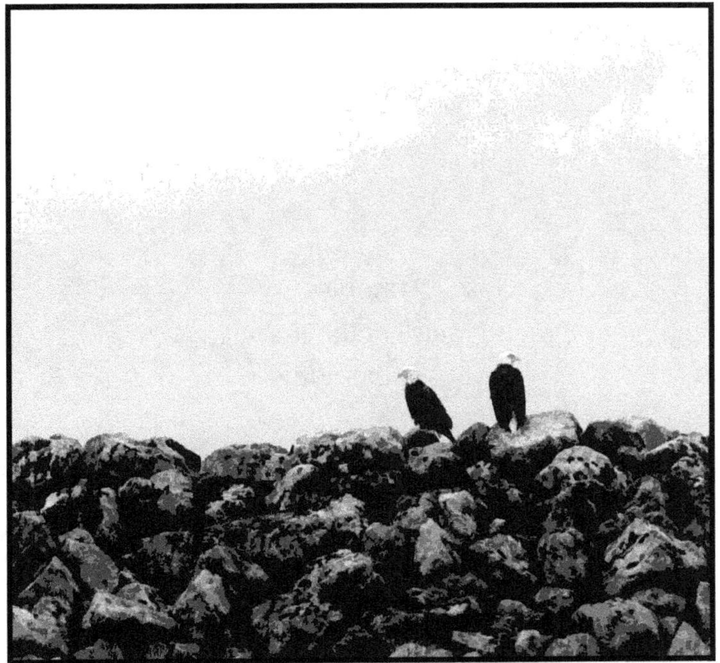

rainbow–
smell of the storm
evaporating

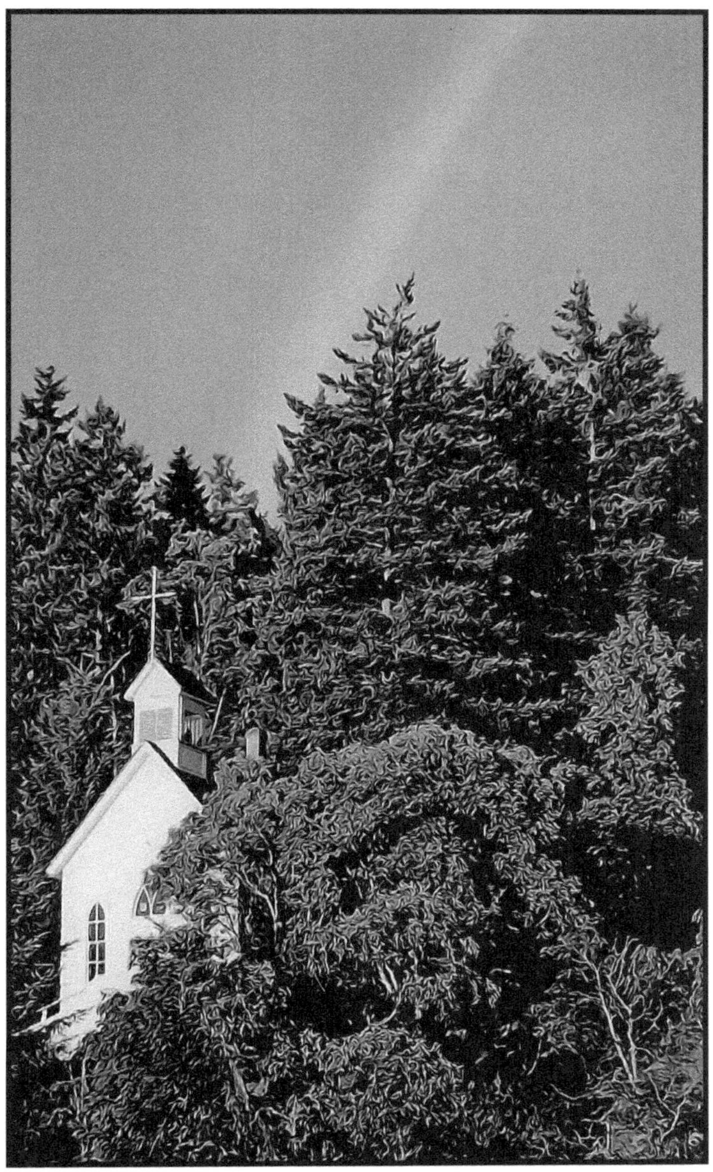

sea lions,
the squawks, the stench–
quick portside turn

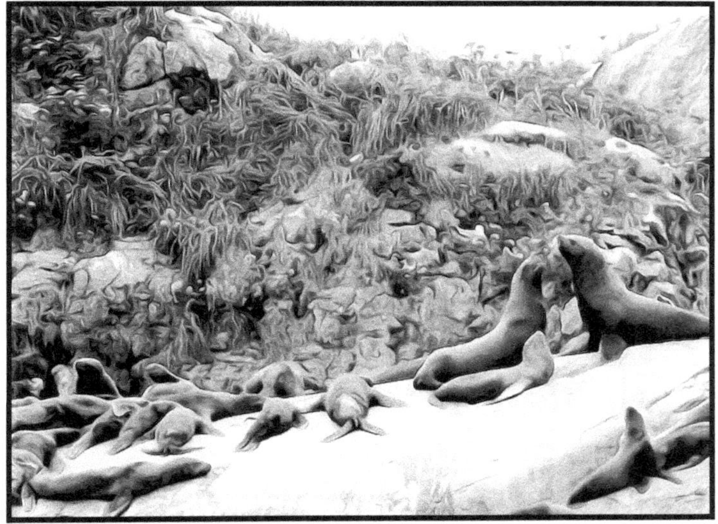

emerge
from the sedge
nose quivering

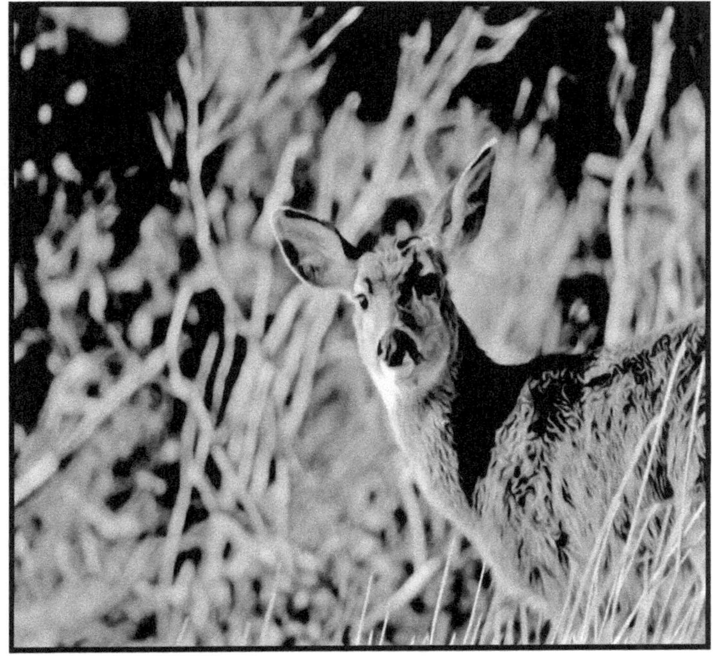

set the anchor,
inhale
the hush

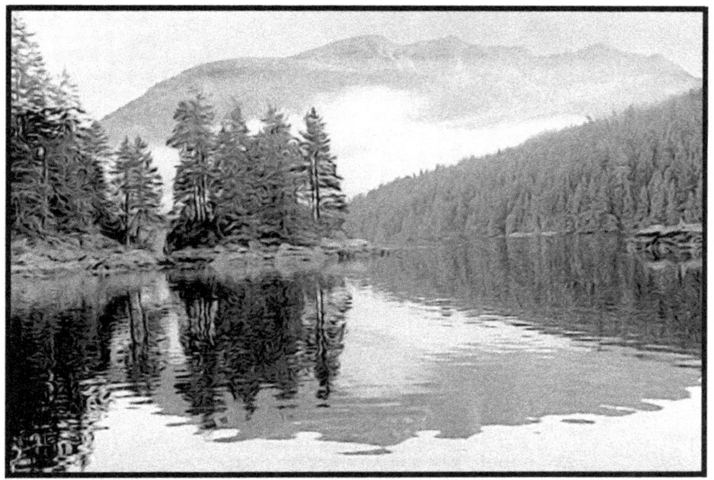

this vast cove–
a gaggle of goslings
corralled

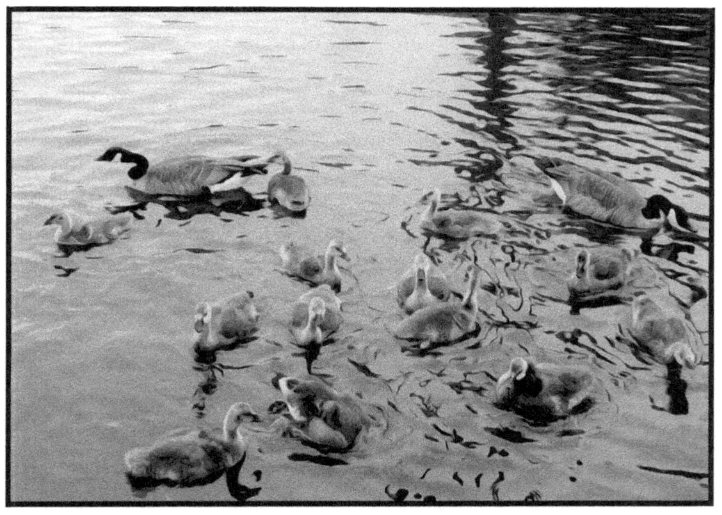

deserted fjord
tall walls
tell tall tales

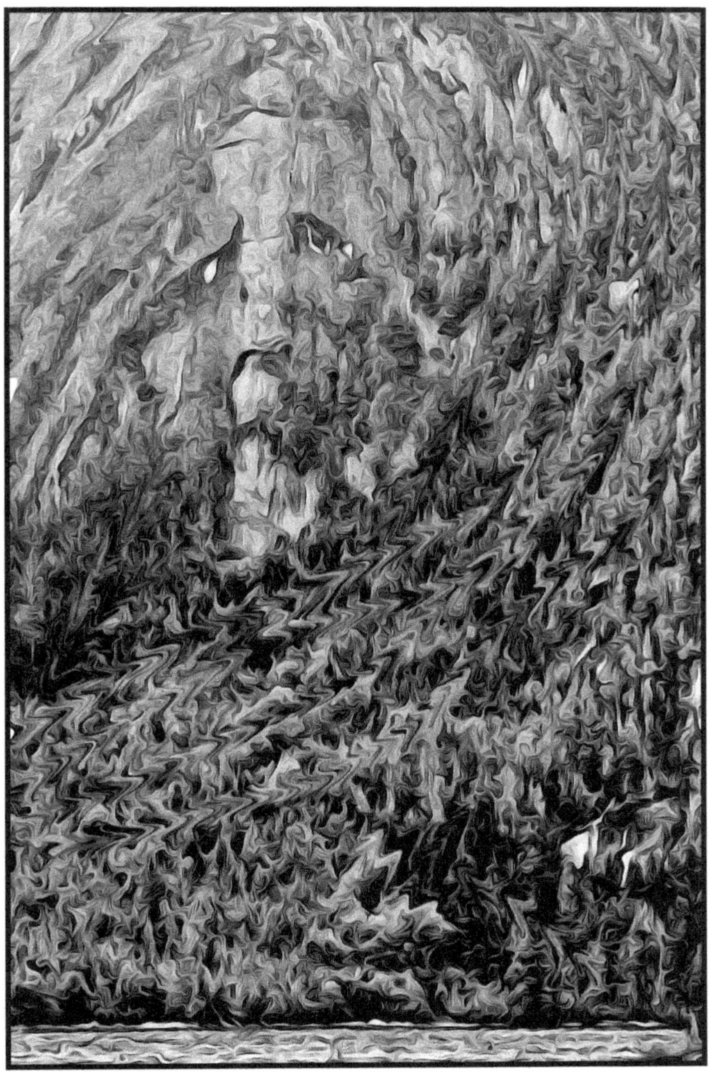

Sally Stiles

Chatham Strait
orca dives into
the rumble of water

with apologies to the master, Basho

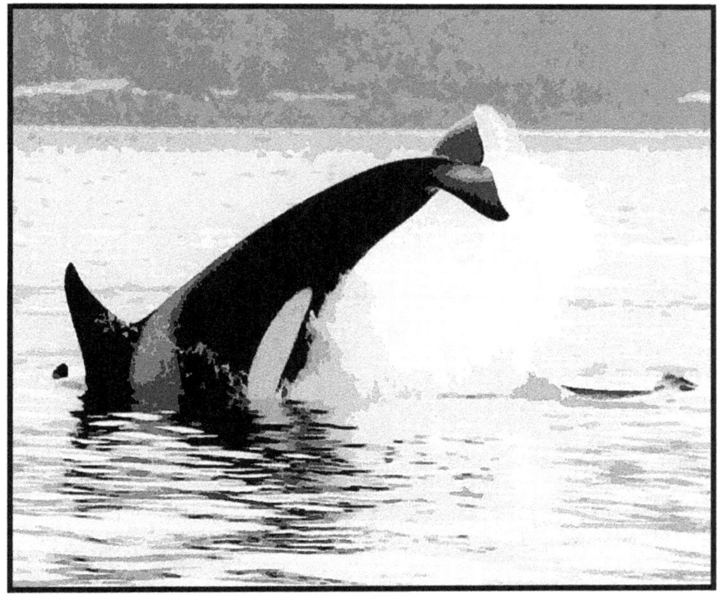

approach Ketchikan
add a final flag
to the pole

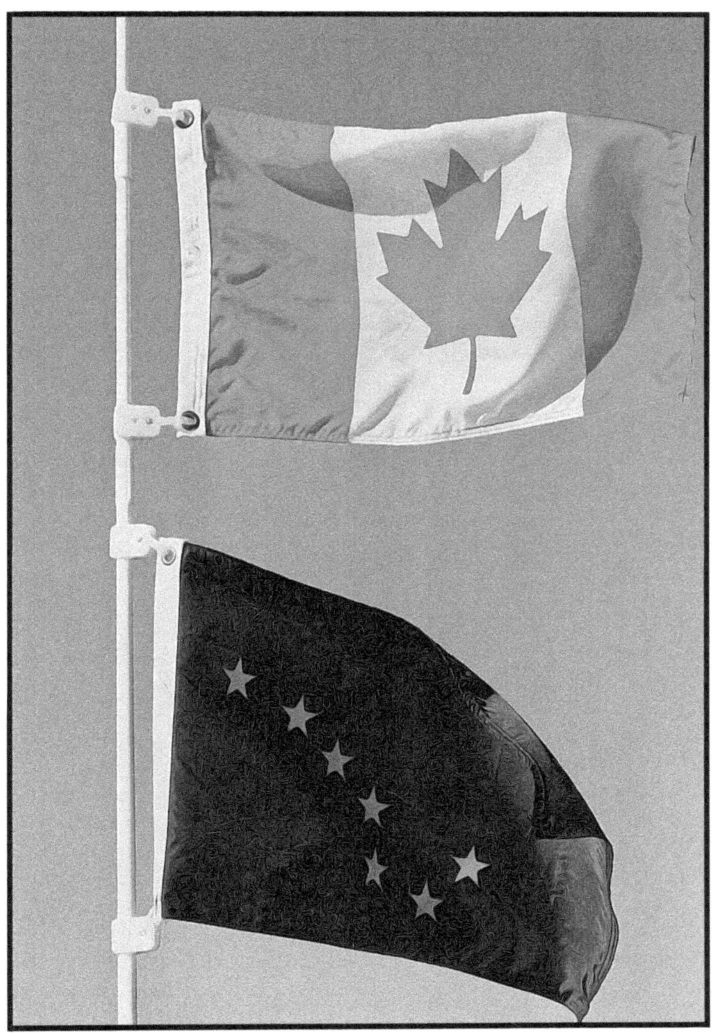

gentle rain
all but mosquitoes
napping

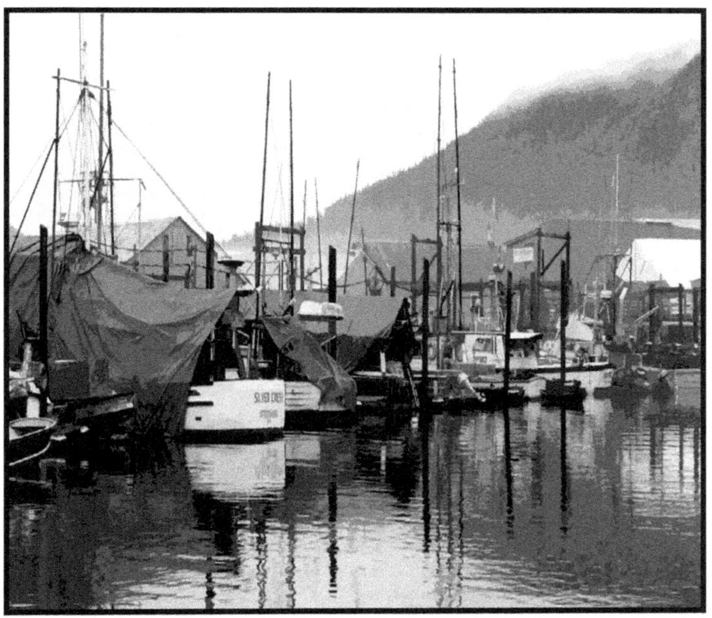

4th of July:
bears join in
a morning swim

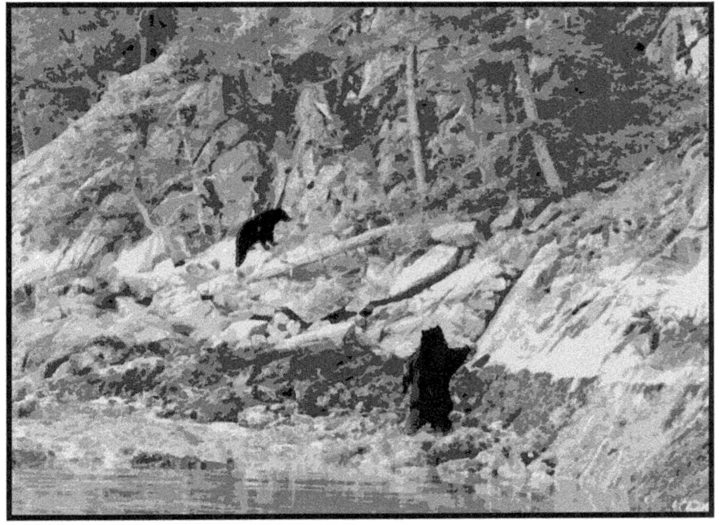

fishing boat creaks
against the dock—
a cradlesong recalled

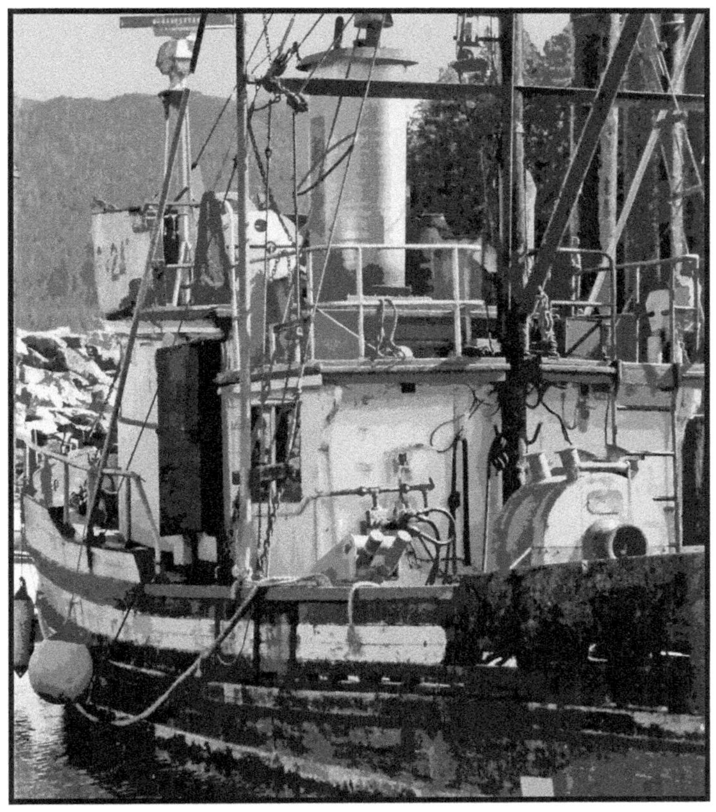

into a haiku
about a gnarled tree
an eagle lands

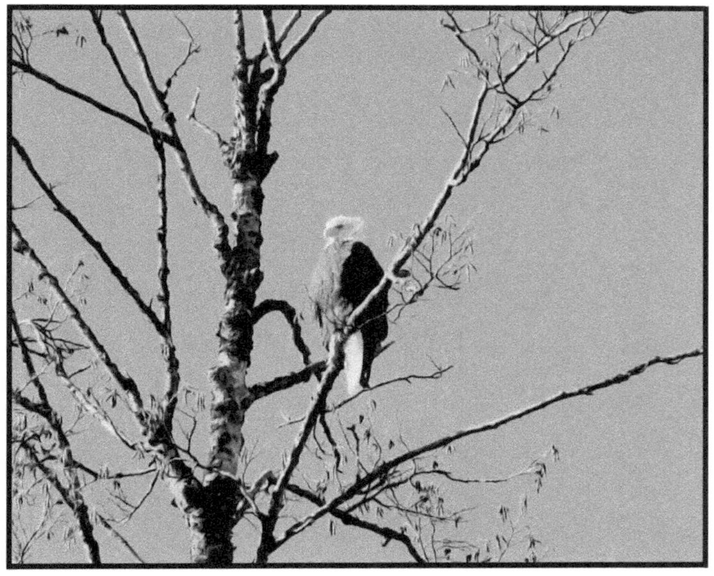

even the paths
beneath the cedars
whisper as we walk

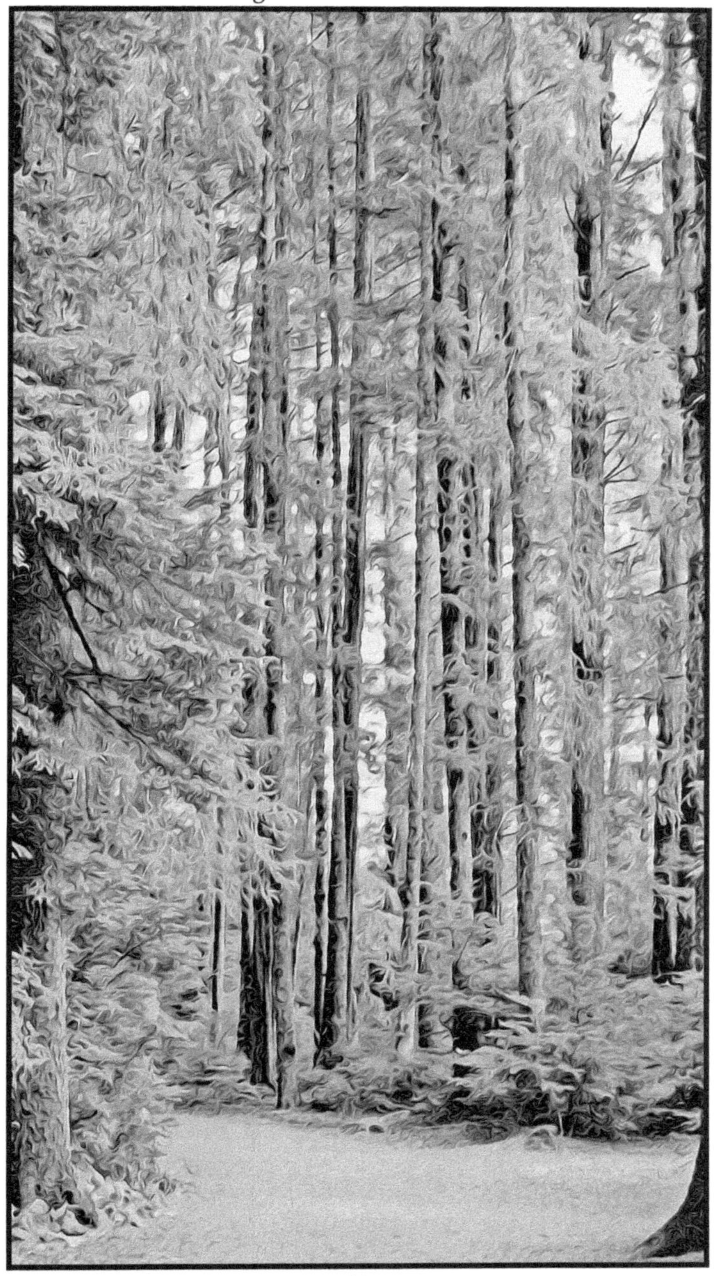

raven, eagle, chief
ancestral sprirts
summoned

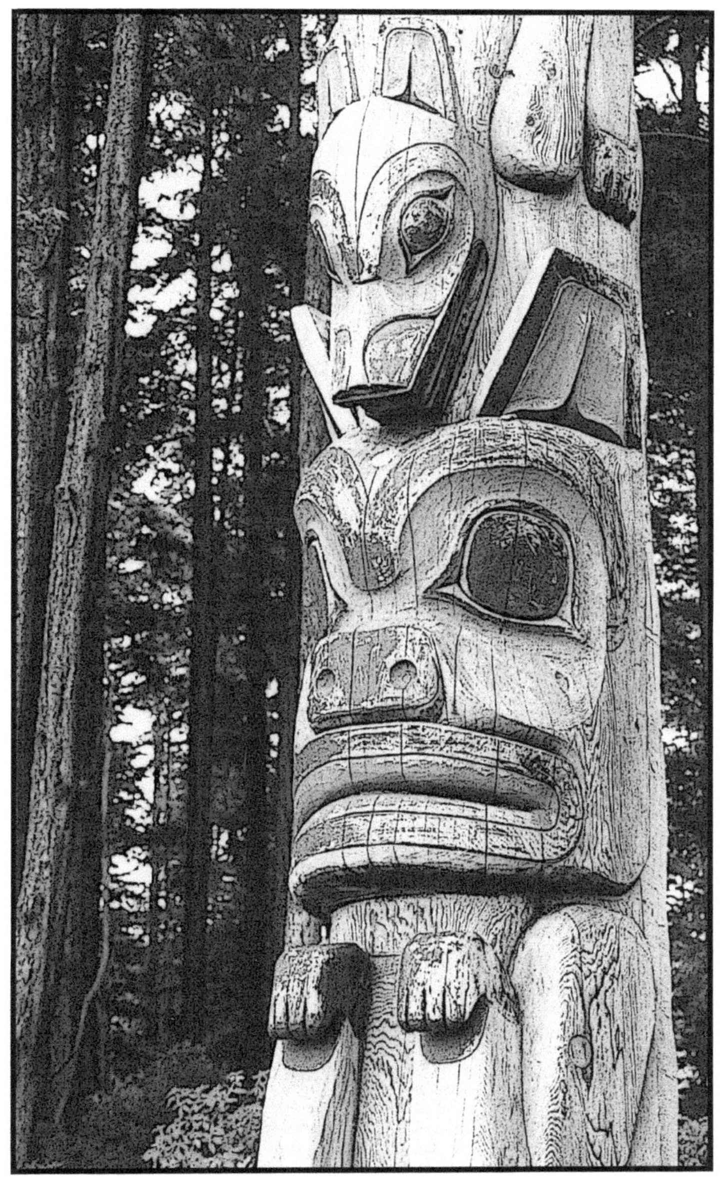

the birds, the whales,
the oncoming tide—
salmon run

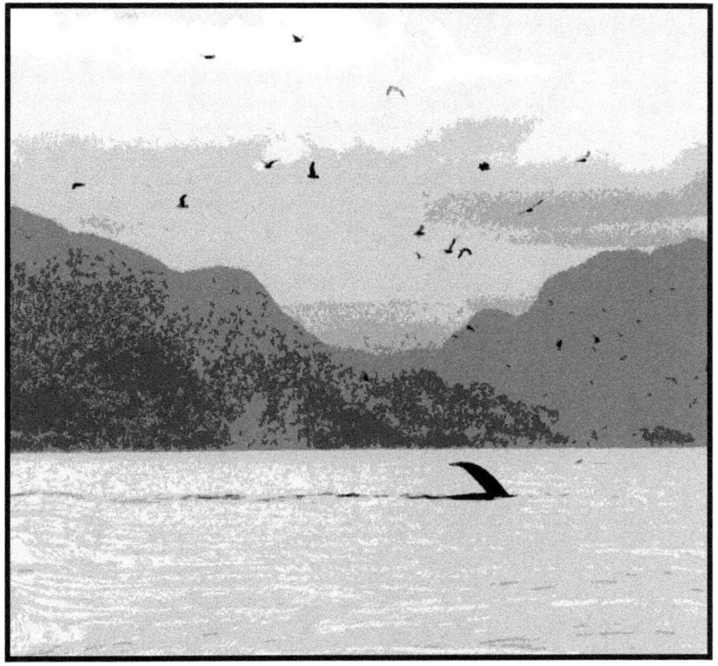

Sunday morning:
contemplate the creation
of a mountain peak

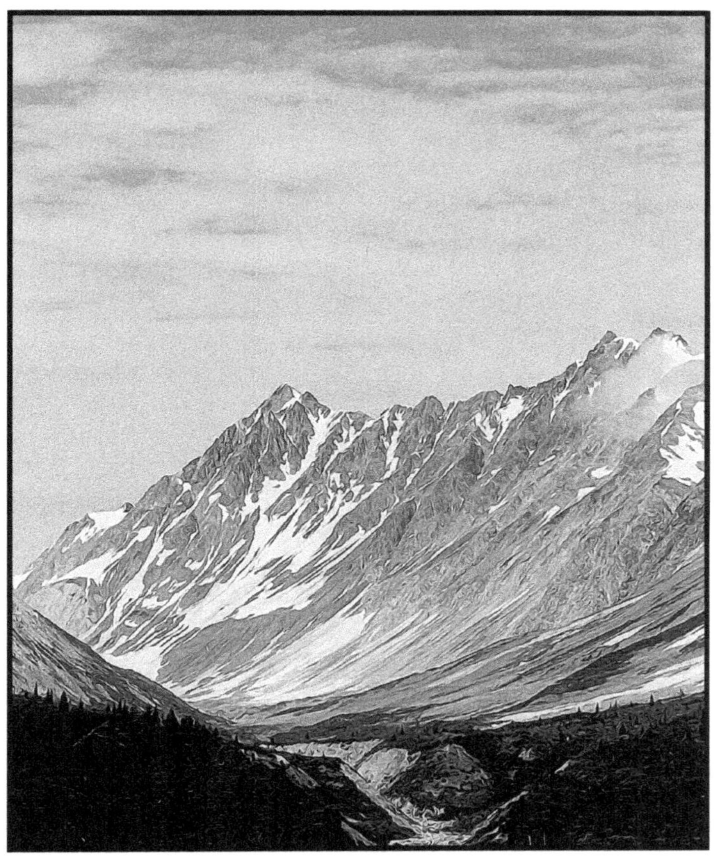

drift ice–
three gullls
hop the ferry

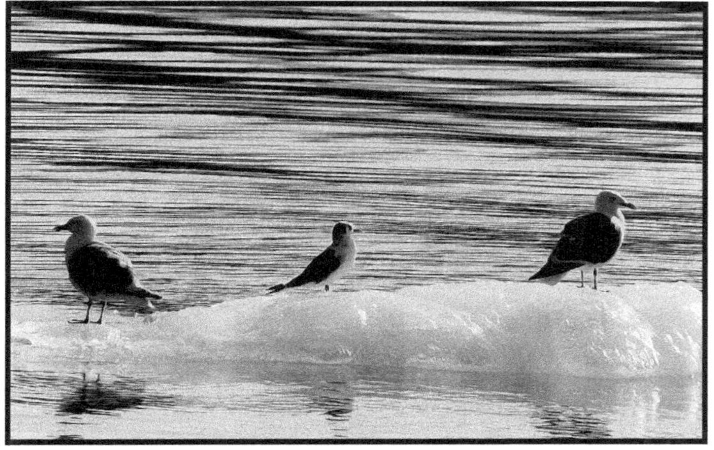

supermoon tonight–
dinghy swings
to the drum of the waves

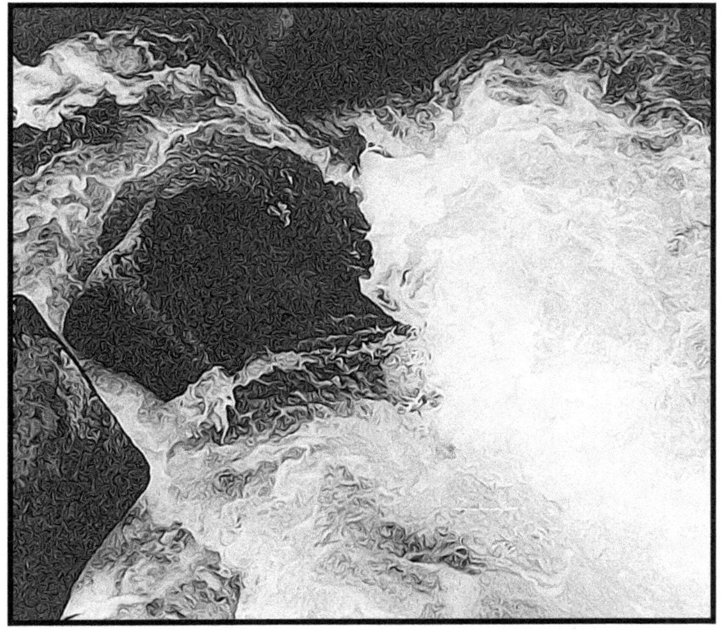

fish for fish
fishing
for fish

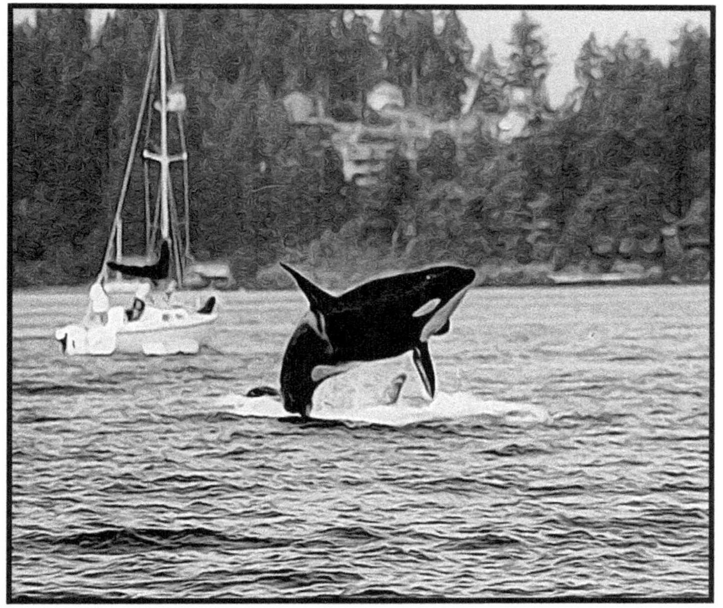

hummingbird–
the beat of
an old jazz tune

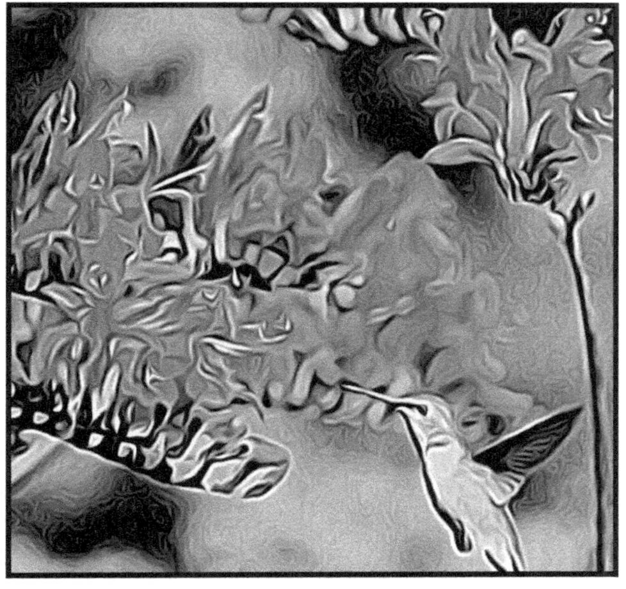

twilight:
high-stepping the shallows,
a great blue heron

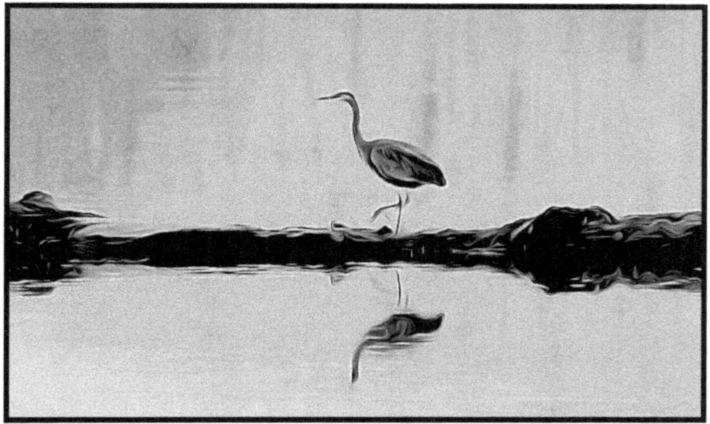

first of September—
summer's fog
lingers on

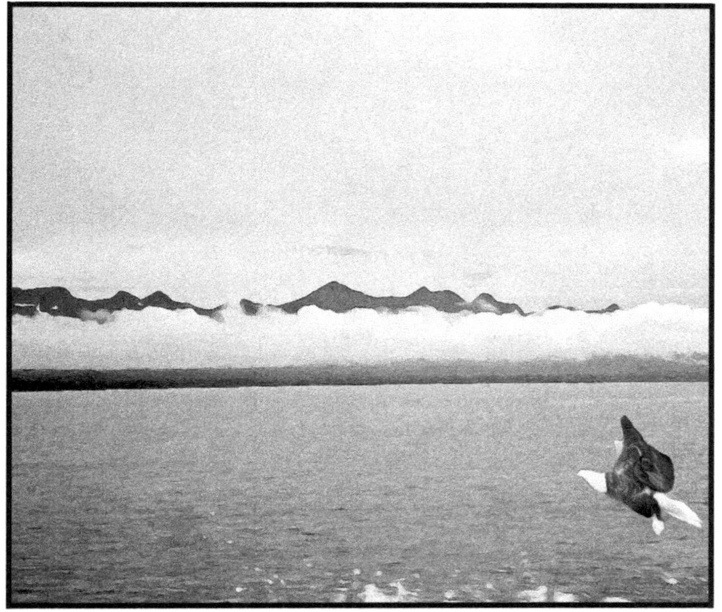

over the yardarm
the sun dips into
the sun

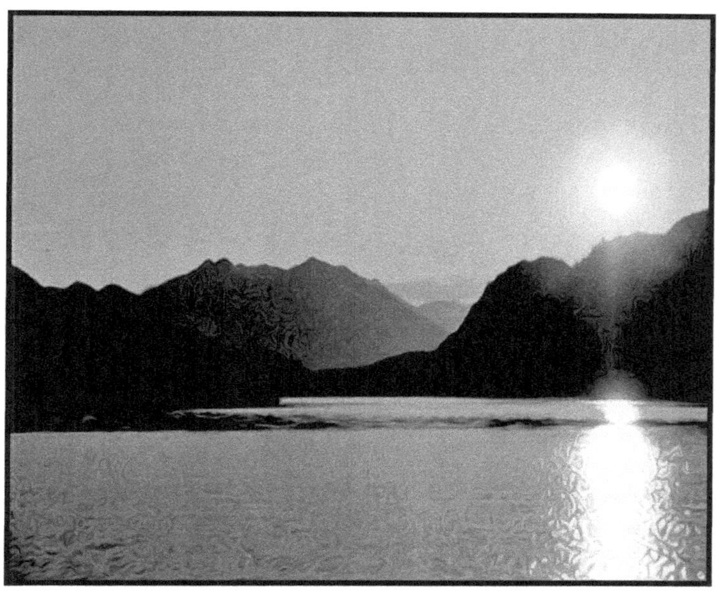

nearing the cascade
can you hear
the silence?

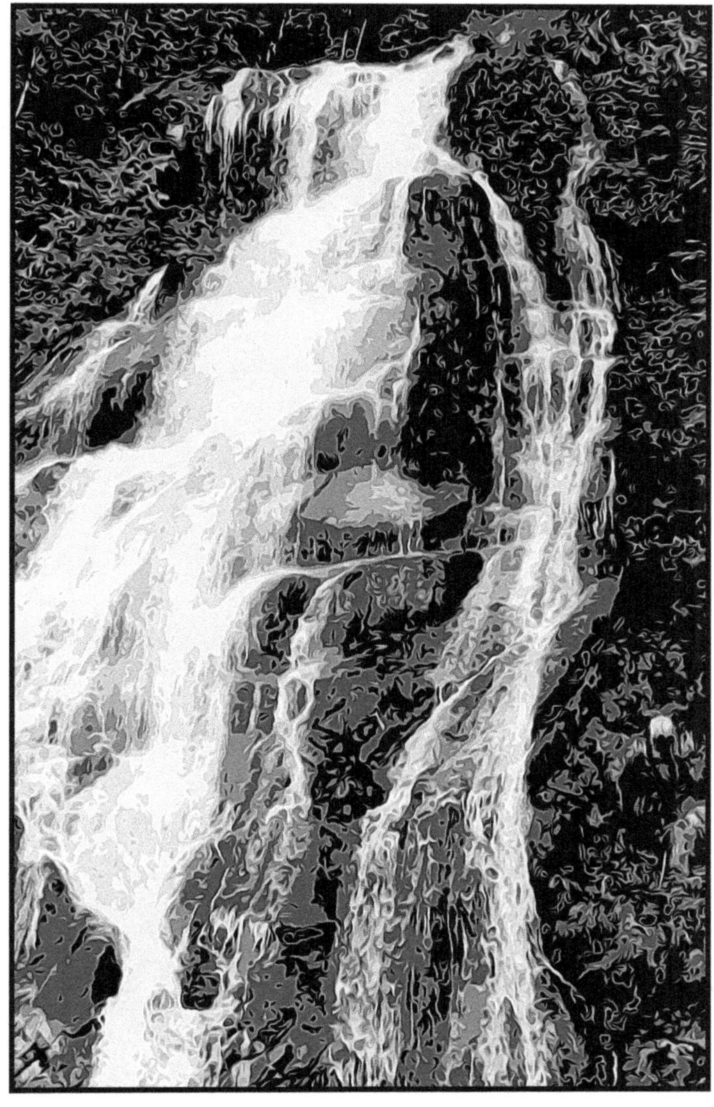

turning home—
what memories trail
in our wake

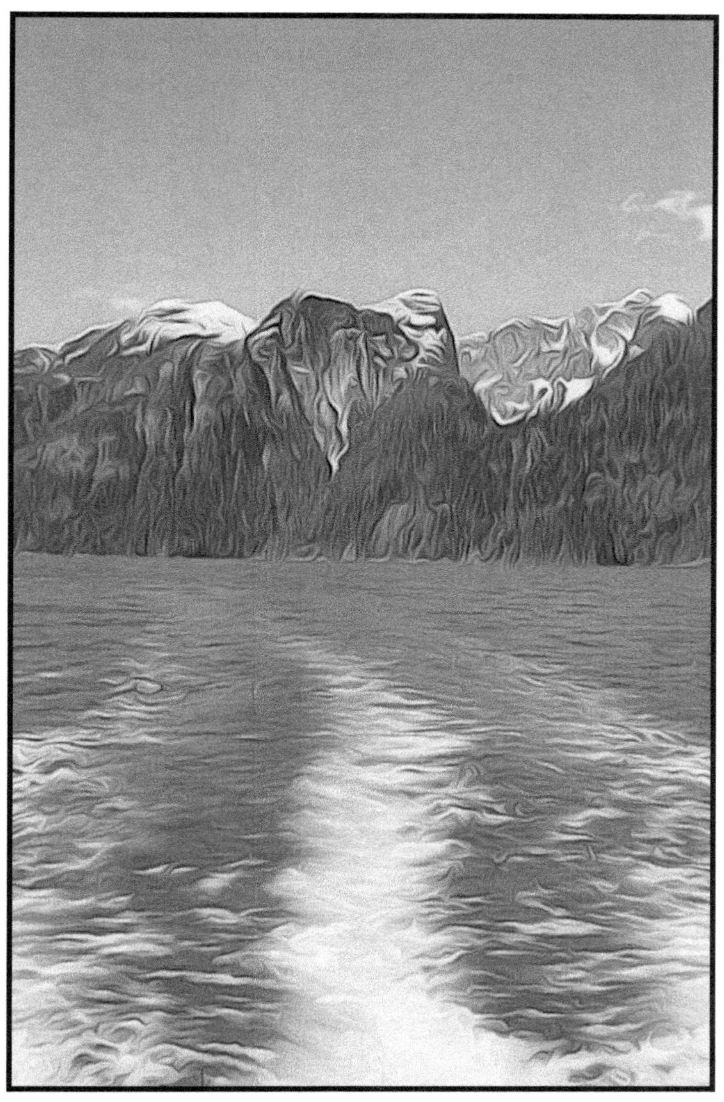

THANK YOU

Every book draws upon other talents
to reach its potential.
I am grateful for
Dalia Pagani, Nicole Chen, John Conlee, Kathleen Jabs,
Greg Lilly, Katheryn Lovell, Shelley Roeder and James Tobin

and especially

for David--
dreams beyond dreams
can come true

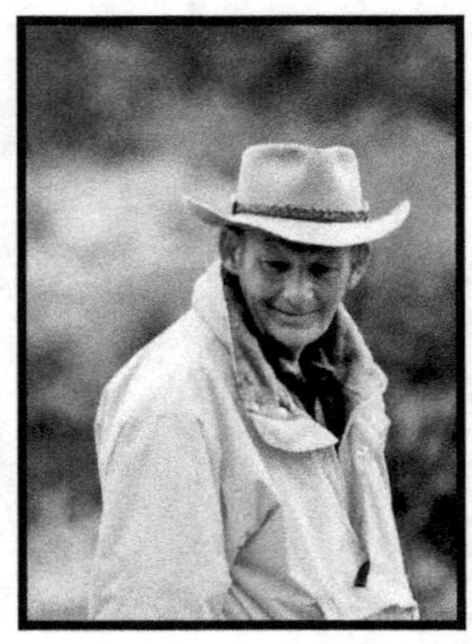

www.ingramcontent.com/pod-product-compliance
Lightning Source LLC
LaVergne TN
LVHW010108110826
845155LV00028B/541